FUNDRAISING FOR DEANS

A GUIDE

———————

JAMES M. LANGLEY

———————

ACADEMIC IMPRESSIONS | 2014
DENVER, CO

Published by Academic Impressions.

CR Mrig Company. 4601 DTC Blvd., Suite 800, Denver, CO 80237.

Copyright © 2014 James Langley.

Cover design by Brady Stanton.

For reproduction, distribution, or copy permissions, or to order additional copies, please contact the Academic Impressions office at 720.488.6800 or visit:

http://bit.ly/2qbHuLr

Academic Impressions

ISBN: 978-1-948658-04-1

Printed in the United States of America.

OTHER BOOKS YOU MAY ENJOY

Fundraising for Deans: A Guide is one of a set of of four groundbreaking fundraising guides for university leaders written by James Langley. The others are:

- *Fundraising for Deans*
- *Fundraising for Boards*
- *Comprehensive Fundraising Campaigns: A Guide for Presidents and Boards*

Securing your institution's financial future isn't just about raising more dollars — it's about creating the conditions that foster continued and increased support. These four books rethink how your president, board members, academic deans, and other key stakeholders support the work of fundraising and donor relationship building. Learn practical strategies for involving those stakeholders at every stage of the donor lifecycle.

"This is is a treasure trove of great advice, forward-thinking reflections, and the tough, but much needed questions that presidents, boards, vice presidents and deans need to ask one another before embarking on a fundraising campaign." - *Matthew T. Lambert, Vice President for University Advancement, William & Mary*

Get all of James Langley's fundraising guides at:

https://www.academicimpressions.com/product/jim-langleys-fundraising-guides-university-leaders/

CONTENTS

STARTING RIGHT

You've just been named dean of the College. Congratulations. No doubt you feel reasonably well suited to the task. After all, you have achieved a measure of distinction in the tripartite expectations of your field—in teaching, research and service. You acquitted yourself quite well in a highly competitive search and were deemed to have the best vision, leadership style, and temperament to meet the demands of the job.

The only area where you may feel less than fully prepared and therefore confident is in the area of fundraising. The subject of fundraising came up frequently in your interview process. Some faculty groused about how far current fundraising efforts had fallen short of their expectations while others gleefully imagined how much more productive it would no doubt be under your tenure. The provost and president spent a great deal of time quizzing you about it—stressing its importance and inquiring as to your willingness to pursue it with vigor.

You have some familiarity with fundraising, of course. You have given numerous talks at various alumni gatherings over the years and have met with donors at university events. And, from all you can tell, it's not exactly rocket science. There's certainly nothing particularly challenging about the terminology of the field. The AVP in central advancement stresses performance metrics and seems to be cajoling everyone under him to "meet their numbers." Your presumption is that if they do as he urges, results will be ever rosier. The development officer in your college says, "it's all about relationships" which sounds like an unimpeachable, if unquantifiable, assumption. So you wonder about the conjunction of metrics and relationships.

You note, however, that your new colleagues, the other deans, manifest a variety of styles and approaches. The business school dean is viewed as aggressive, opportunistic, eager to ask, and willing to "challenge" prospects to do more than they might otherwise. The dean of humanities, on the other hand, says she has achieved great success through her advisory council and by taking time with each significant prospect to "bring them along." You wonder which of these approaches, or more subtle variations of them, would be most productive.

Further, the advice you receive on the subject also runs the gamut. A prominent alumnus urges you to take the time to listen and to get to know people. The chair of the advisory board you inherited stresses the need for you to be "out there" as a visible, confident, enthusiastic fundraiser. Several successful business people on that board stress that you be "active in fundraising." You listen to all of them and then resolve the best way to learn is by doing.

The College's development officer (or DO, as he is commonly referred to) has received mixed marks during your search process. Some say he's fallen well short of the promises he made when being considered for the job. Others say he worked hard but was hamstrung by your predecessor, who had come to be caustically characterized as being "all send, no receive." Still others blamed byzantine bureaucracy of the central development, and the president's propensity to poach your best development prospects.

You decide it only reasonable to give your DO a chance and see how he does. You set up a meeting to seek his advice on how you can get started. You assume he will have you on the fabled "rubber chicken circuit" before long, if not orchestrating some heady opportunities—perhaps making a case in a corporate boardroom, hobnobbing at a private golf club, or sipping expensive wine at sumptuous dinners with avid donors in tony eateries.

GETTING STARTED

If he's a very good DO, he will come to that first meeting prepared to focus your subsequent efforts on the two essential parts of the fundraising equation: **case** and **connection**, or "What do we hope to raise money for, and who is most apt to support the project?" For the time being, let's focus on your potential sources of support, or your connections.

Connecting with Your Development Officer

Your DO should come to your first meeting with an in-depth analysis of the College's prospect pool. That pool should be tiered according to those who have the highest capacity and propensity to give.

- **Capacity** will have be determined by some sort of "wealth screening" or scan of public records to determine each prospect's net worth, if not the make-up of their assets.

- **Propensity** will have been assessed primarily by a review of each prospect's philanthropic history. Ideally, that giving will have been to your college or university. If not, a record of giving elsewhere still suggests that you will be dealing with someone who feels grateful for what life has provided and possesses a corollary commitment to giving back.

If your DO comes with a list of names, absent an analytical rationale for their ordering, you should ask for the rationale before proceeding. The absence of analytics will make it very difficult to determine who you should see first, why, and what you should say. Yes, the judgment of a DO and the experience borne from it is of immense value, but the art of fundraising is not without science. You should see evidence of both art and science.

The art of fundraising is not without science.

Your DO should be able to articulate the criteria that was applied to the shaping of the list, including how the giving potential of each prospect was calculated. He or she should point out that calculations of individual net worth are based only on aggregations of public records (real estate deeds, stock purchases, significant acquisitions and sales, etc.) and whatever your development operation has been able to glean from the prospects themselves (and they are often remarkably open about the subject).

Further, your development officer should explain that capacity ratings, the estimate of what a prospect might give, is based on a formula (usually 5% of his or her net worth) but that such ratings are only given under certain circumstances.

The preponderance of your prospects and the focus of most of those analytics should be individuals, not foundations or corporations.

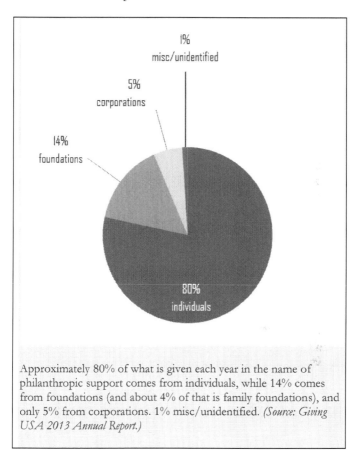

Approximately 80% of what is given each year in the name of philanthropic support comes from individuals, while 14% comes from foundations (and about 4% of that is family foundations), and only 5% from corporations. 1% misc/unidentified. *(Source: Giving USA 2013 Annual Report.)*

If your school or college is more technical, you may see a larger percentage of your support coming from corporations than is the national norm, but spending most of your time on individuals is almost always the most productive strategy. Here's why: corporations give to achieve corporate objectives, and, according to numerous interviews I have conducted with corporate leaders, the foremost among their reasons for giving to educational institutions are:

1. To improve their ability to identify and recruit talented graduates.

2. To glean knowledge from faculty research that will aid in business development.

3. To sell their products to students in hopes of forming lifelong habits.

Corporate support, therefore, can be more market sensitive and can change as leadership and businesses' strategies shift.

Foundation support, particularly that which comes from the large, national powerhouses, is given along programmatic lines, usually to support internally developed and strongly held beliefs. The Gates or Lumina Foundation, for instance, has given magnificently in the name of educational reform but they have clear ideas, based on their own research and practice, on how it is best achieved. The Kauffman Foundation, to cite another example, has very firm beliefs on the best ways to advance entrepreneurship. The viability of any proposal you may submit to them will not rest entirely on the strength of your arguments or the proof of your capabilities but on your ability to demonstrate how you can work within their guidelines to achieve their goals. It is best that you know what makes them tick.

Individuals also come with strong belief systems and preconceived notions as to where their philanthropic support can have the greatest impact. Yet, individuals will become more trusting of institutions through substantive interactions with leaders, with ROI- oriented stewardship, and through the benefit of time. The longer an individual gives to an institution, in general, the more apt they are to see it as an extension of their values and purposes. And the individuals that are most likely to manifest these qualities are your grateful beneficiaries, also known as alumni. In fact, there is no more predictable, probable source of significant giving—be it for major, principal or estate gifts—than loyal individuals. The more consecutive years they give to your school or institution, the greater those probabilities.

There is no more predictable, probable source of significant giving—be it for major, principal or estate gifts—than loyal individuals.

Indeed, one of the wisest actions you can take in your early days as dean is not only to ask for a list of the twenty-five largest gifts to your school, but to ask, in each case, the number of years donors previously gave to the school before those large gifts were received. If the average number of years is less than ten, your donors are highly anomalous. While there is no single source for the data, various analyses conducted in recent years at multiple institutions suggest the average number of years preceding a gift of $1 million is twelve to fifteen.

If the prospect list you are presented is analytically sound, you can begin to plan which prospects you should see and in what order. You might be wondering if you should ask these prospects to support the college at the first meeting, either in broad or specific terms. Chances are you should not. Based on Langley Innovations' multiple- year analyses of over forty successful fundraising universities, I can add that even when dealing with the best of prospects, it takes, on average, twenty-one months and nine interactions to secure a major gift. Even if you have a subset of prospects who had been highly engaged with the previous dean but never asked for a gift, it doesn't mean that they are ready or prepared for you to ask them. The only exception would be those prospects who had been in discussion with your predecessor about a particular project or initiative, say an endowed chair. If there had been a series of discussions about that chair and a specific gift amount had been discussed but never committed to, you could broach the topic to determine how you might pick up and advance those negotiations.

> *Even when dealing with the best of prospects, it takes, on average, twenty-one months and nine interactions to secure a major gift.*

Yet, even when you have inherited strong prospects who have been discussing specific commitments with the previous dean, you should look at another set of facts— the dates of the last two interactions with each. If your DO insists, for instance, that a particular couple is "just waiting" to be asked, but you see that the last visit with them was five months ago, and the visit before that six months before the previous visit, you should resist. If gift negotiations are proceeding positively, no more than six to eight weeks should elapse between interactions. It is not dissimilar to a romance: the more often two people see each other, the more time they spend together, and the more commonalities they find, the more it suggests they will commit to a future together. The implications of the inverse are obvious.

But, the overarching point is this: your development plan needs to be built on a clear-eyed assessment of the field of prospects you have inherited. For instance:

- If you inherit a large number of well-developed relationships, including a healthy number of alumni and friends with years of giving under their belts, you can broach the subject of fundraising in your early interactions with them.

- If the vast majority of your prospects have not interacted for any length of time with your school and/or those interactions have not been recent, you should avoid rushing into a selling or even an institutional advocacy mode. It would be far wiser to ask the prospect's personal, civic, or profess-ional aspirations to see if there is a potential of aligning purposes somewhere down the road.

In other words, the style of fundraising that one might adapt—forthright or patient—should be determined by the strength and recentness of the relationship with the prospect.

Understanding the Dean's Role

While some fundraising relationships between dean and donor become personal, they should begin on a professional level. The dean's role in building such a relationship is to:

- Define the highest and most enduring purposes of the school/ college.

- Determine, through research and planning, where additional resources will allow the school/ college to give students a jump on the future, or to serve society through the application of new knowledge or responsive service.

- Explain where and how specific levels of investment can achieve those specific goals.

- Listen to donor interests and intentions and frame gift agreements that align purposes and manage expectations.

- Report in a frank, factual, and timely way on progress made or unexpected obstacles.

- Share successes and honor service of experienced faculty, staff, students, and volunteers.

While there are many other niceties that will help cement more personal bonds, none of them will substitute for these professional responsibilities. Conversely, their fulfillment will generate the most valuable form of advertising—word of mouth praise from a discerning investor.

Understanding the Case for Support

The second pillar of successful fundraising is the case for support. In an increasingly competitive world—one that has a growing number of philanthropy-seeking organizations with ever larger fundraising staffs clamoring for ever more support—a distinctive, compelling, strategic case for support has become of the utmost importance. The elements of the most effective cases are clear, factual, content- rich elucidations of:

- A gap analysis that defines, in specific, factual, and compelling terms, the gap between the current level of service being provided and what the future will demand. This will ensure, for example, that the school's graduates are adequately equipped and prepared for the greatest opportunities and obligations they will face;

- Where the formulation and delivery of new knowledge, service, or innovation can improve the human condition in concrete ways; or

- How a particular service, based on a particularly rich competence, can ameliorate a problem and/or create a virtuous societal circle.

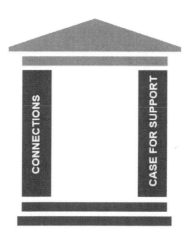

ACTIVITY: ASSESS YOUR CURRENT CASE FOR SUPPORT

Do you have your case for support on hand? Is it clearly articulated? Does it incorporate the preceding three points? If not, gather your staff and begin to work through these questions. Also, be sure to seek alumni and prospect input.

Examples include:

- A school of education at a prominent public university seeking funding to create a model charter school because fewer and fewer graduates of the local public high schools are qualifying for admission.

- A business school seeking support to create a cadre of consultants from its current and future faculty to provide practical advice to fledging companies in its host city.

- A school of psychiatry/psychology proposing to create training, mentoring, and support to counselors in local schools who are overwhelmed by a growing host of emotional struggles that manifest in their students.

- A college of liberal arts striving to respond to a spiking demand from students and employers for more competence in Mandarin and Arabic by creating new class sections, relevant study abroad, and "cultural internships" that will ensure both language and cultural proficiency upon graduation.

- An engineering school proposing to establish practical internships and problem-solving sessions with nonprofits to give their students real-life opportunities and to provide nonprofits with a skillset that they, all too often, fall short of.

ACTIVITY, CONTINUED

- A library is armed with the results of a study correlating student academic success with the number of hours spent each week in the library in study groups. It is proposing to create a honeycomb of study group nodes by adding a wing equipped with wireless capability and increased reference librarian services. The new wing would be designed with large windows for students walking by to see the scholarly, social activity within and feel induced to join in.

Understanding Donor Psychology

As you consider these kinds of possibilities, and imagine ways that you can leverage the unique capabilities of your school to address issues of great external import, you may find yourself wondering, "Yes, but what about the bread and butter of what we do; what about funding for core purposes?" Well, fundraising is about the alignment of internal expectations with external realities. One such reality is a culturally entrenched but unwritten compact. It is lodged in the psychology of philanthropists. It is the widely held belief that philanthropy is not about responding to emergencies or the underwriting of everyday functions and purposes, but about providing the margin of excellence, about taking an organization, or some part of it, from good to great. Philanthropy, in the minds of many who give and those who give the most, is not about the margin of survival or making recipients happy, or creating

Lake Woebegones or social utopias. It is about leveraging existing strength to create even greater strength.

Fundraising is about the alignment of internal expectations with external realities.

Yes, people do give to pressing social needs, natural disasters, and humanitarian efforts. Those are acts of charity. But the plain and simple truth is that people give far less in the name of charity than they do for philanthropic purposes. They will, in short, give less "to give a man a fish" and far more to anything that "teaches him how to fish."

And, yes, there are those who give to core purposes of schools, colleges, and universities, but, in the vast majority of cases, they come from long and/or deeply involved alumni who give at modest levels. The more one is apt to give, the more one wants to know that he or she is not "throwing good money after bad." Donors want to know that their gifts are building strength and improving delivery systems, not patching up flawed, outdated systems or perpetuating mediocre performance. Grateful, debt-free, actively engaged graduates of private colleges may be more inclined to give unrestricted gifts to support their alma maters, but their numbers are in decline in the vast majority of cases. In fact, higher education's most likely source of significant and sustained support— their alumni—has been eroding for the past twenty years. When contributing alumni of the top 100 institutions of higher learning in the U.S. were asked why they did not give more to their alma maters, the most common reasons, according to a study done by Engagement Strategies Group, were:

- I feel that I have paid enough already for tuition.

- I don't think the school really needs the money.

- I haven't been given a good enough reason to give.

- I don't feel a deep emotional connection to the school.

- They haven't done enough to connect with me beyond asking for money.

- I feel like donations go into a "black hole."

As you can see, the making of a strong case for private support entails anticipating and overcoming these concerns and objections. In the past quarter century, four-year institutions of higher learning increased tuition by 440%, according to the National Center for Public Policy and Higher Education. As they did, more and more alumni began asking, "If you're getting that much from tuition revenue why do you need private support, particularly for core purposes?" So, in making a broad case for private support, it is wise to explain that while tuition dollars are used primarily for core purposes, private dollars may be used to strengthen select initiatives or further amplify key capabilities. Tuition dollars should work hand-in-hand with private support. Conflating the two or failing to explain how tuition dollars can be leveraged by private support will weaken your ability to make a case for the latter, to build credibility with prospects, and to win the support of generous but discerning donors.

THE APPOINTMENT WITH A PROSPECT OR DONOR: DOS AND DON'TS

Now that you've grasped the core concepts, you're eager to move forward and engage your very best prospects. The way you go about seeking the appointments, the tone you set when you meet prospects, the subject matter with which you engage them, the level of discourse you encourage, and the manner in which you listen and respond will determine whether doors that open once will do so again. In other words, do all you can to harness the power of the positive first impression. The following is a step-by-step guide to direct your initial and ongoing interactions with prospects and donors.

Before the Appointment

1. ***Do* personalize the request for the first appoint-ment:** Requests for prospect appoint-ments should come from you, not your development officer (DO). If they come from the DO, it sends the signal of how you intend to define the relationship. The vast majority of the prospects you meet, many of whom will be current or past donors, understand that the conversation will get around to fundraising at some point. However, they will be hoping that you will value and find outlets for their values,

talents, experience, know-how, and wisdom. You can request these appointments using email or the phone. These are prospects with whom you hope to build lasting relationships, so the more personal attention and courtesy you can afford, the better.

2. ***Do* make the request for the right reasons**: Establish yourself at the outset as a listener. Make it clear, as a new dean, that you are engaged in a listening exercise and seeking the advice and counsel to ensure that you formulate a truly strategic plan for your school or college

3. ***Do* reassure them of your intentions**: Since so many alumni and other prospects have come to believe that every request from their alma mater will be about fundraising, no matter the pretext, you may find it necessary to assure some prospects that you are *not* coming to seek their support, in order to secure an appointment with them. Whenever possible, make it clear that your first priority is to build a web of strategic relationships and establish common cause with civic and business leaders. You don't want to mislead and act as if you will never ask for their support. You can make it clear that you're not a quick-hit artist; that you know their support has to be earned; and that you are willing to take the time to listen, to align purposes, and to find common cause before soliciting their support.

4. ***Do* choose the right vehicle and venue of engagement:** In most instances, you should demonstrate respect by offering to meet your top prospects at their office, home, private club, or place of their choosing. Initial meetings should be one-on-one, without a development officer, once again to demonstrate that you seek to build more

than a one-dimensional relationship. Be willing to meet your prospects at times of their choosing. Don't feel compelled to invite them to lunches or dinners, or to wine and dine them at elegant restaurants. If they are truly top prospects, they don't need you to buy them a nice meal or an expensive bottle of wine. You won't win over a prospect by being lavish in your entertainments; if anything, you may cause them to believe that you must have an abundance of resources.

If you are visiting prospects in other cities, you may have to build some appointments around meals. If you offer the invitation to dine, you should pick a very good restaurant while avoiding the posh. If the prospect states a preference for wine, a moderately priced one will be fine. When the check comes, you should pick it up. If the prospect intercepts it, you should let him/her do so, and thank them for allowing you to put the money to academic use.

When you request an appointment, ask for a specific length of time and stick to that timeframe. One hour, or even slightly less, is a reasonable request. It is generally not a good idea to get groups of top prospects together for introductory meetings, as this makes the interaction less personal to the donor.

During the Appointment

5. ***Do* be yourself:** There's no ideal persona that you need to inhabit. The personalities of deans who have been effective   run the gamut, but all are comfortable in their own skin. Simple human

qualities like authenticity, sincerity, and demonstrating a genuine interest in others always win the day. Of course, in all of our cases, shouldn't we be striving to always be better "selves"?

6. ***Do* avoid presumptions:** Even the most loyal donors don't want to be taken for granted. It's never wise to assume that people are just waiting to hear what you need or are wanting the latest news from your school. In an initial meeting, explore the prospect's relationship to your school. Be sure to ask these key questions:

    o "Do you feel as if your previous gift was put to good use?"

    o "Were you properly thanked?"

    o "How did the previous dean relate to you?"

    o "What has been your *most* and *least* rewarding experience with the school?"

    Their responses can be incredibly valuable insights into the existing strengths and weaknesses of your fundraising operation.

7. ***Don't* humor or flatter prospects:** You don't have to ingratiate yourself with prospects to win them over. If you do, they may not be the kind of supporters you want. The stroking they need may be way out of proportion to their giving. Reasonable prospects and donors look for seriousness of purpose and gravitate to service-oriented leaders who seek ways to bring about positive change and improve the human condition.

8. ***Don't* try to wow prospects into philanthropic submission:** The power of persuasion is overstated. The best fundraising deans are not the ones with the most charismatic personalities or those that paint the most alluring picture or those who overawe their listeners. Indeed, deans who go too hard in that direction cause many prospects to wonder, "If everything is going so well, why do you need my money?" Newcomers to fundraising, believing donors give to reward achievement, strive mightily to impress their philanthropic listeners with the achievements and distinctions of their schools. They fail to realize that donors are seeking to make a difference, to invest in things that bring about substantive and lasting improvements. Effective fundraisers listen to their potential sources of support and find ways to align the aspirations of the school with the passions and values of their supporters.

9. ***Do* confide:** One of the best ways to forge an inner circle of significant supporters is to take them into your confidence, to share what you hope to achieve and the higher level of service you hope to render. Tell them where you see the way forward and where you expect to meet difficulty. Share your doubts and struggles. Be candid about the skills that you offer and the ones that you are missing. This is how you will make prospects feel valued and needed, and how you will recruit them to your cause. The sagest of fundraising deans either intuitively grasp or come to learn this simple fact; the best way to induce giving is to recruit and make effective use of a prospect's talents, wisdom, know how, or experience. When prospects are given a clean shot at solving a real problem, they will give generously of their time and talent. And the more they give of those two commodities, the

more they will give of their treasure. But confide only in the struggles and difficulties in advancing your mission, not your frustration with bureaucracy or internal politics. Inviting donors to do your bidding in internal matters is inevitably divisive and unproductive. Deans who are models of professionalism, who subordinate self on behalf of larger purpose, inspire the greatest confidence over time.

10. ***Do* preview next steps:** Prospects will appreciate you making the rounds to seek their advice and counsel before you formulate, announce, and promulgate your larger plans. They will be mystified, if not miffed, if you do not preview the process and explain what you plan to do with the information you are acquiring. For instance, your prospects will feel so much more a part of the process, and be more supportive throughout if you explain that you will:

   ○ ***Gather information and glean advice***, internally and externally, for the first six to eight months.

   ○ ***Synthesize and share that advice*** with them at that point, and outline how it will be incorporated into the shaping of your strategic priorities. Include the tone and ethos of the community of greater purpose that you intend to build, and invite another round of reactions with questions like:

     ▪ "Does this capture the essence of what we discussed?"

     ▪ "Do the imperatives of our plan strike you as strategic, sensible, and attainable?"

- "Have we missed anything of great importance?"

- "What barriers are we likely to encounter in pursuing these plans, and might we convert them into gateways?"

Always remember that no reasonable person expects you to acquiesce to every opinion or even the weight of overall opinion, but they will appreciate the fact that you have sought to understand the lay of the land that you are about to traverse, and that you have asked them to help guide your way.

Also, remember that the development of a major gift takes twenty-one months, on average, and entails nine interactions. Those who successfully solicit gifts at the end of that process have repeatedly elicited the opinions and advice from their prospects along the way.

○ **Share your first formal formulation of the plan** with those you have interviewed, thanking each personally for their contributions along the way. Make it clear that they are now your trusted "insiders," and that you want them to know about this important development, and all ensuing ones, before they are shared more broadly. Being the "first to know," whether the news is good or bad, but especially if it is bad, makes people feel truly trusted and valued. We will return to this theme later when we address the dynamics of community building and promoting greater institutional momentum.

Being the "first to know," whether the news is good or bad, but especially if it is bad, makes people feel truly trusted and valued.

Following the Appointment

11. ***Don't*** try to accomplish too much too soon: Keep your promise and end the appointment on time. That will increase the likelihood of you securing subsequent ones. Even if you think someone is unusually enthusiastic and can be brought along more quickly, it doesn't mean you should seize the moment. Respect the human decision-making rhythms. The reason it takes twenty-one months to secure a major gift is because prospects need to go through a process which involves a series of escalating steps. First, there is a general awareness of something important; then they attach escalating importance to that object (if given sufficient rationale and information), before making a strong personal commitment to it. A general understanding of and respect for donor psychology is essential to deans' fundraising success.

    The ascending steps of commitment that convert prospects to donors likely include some or all of the following:

    - Seeing a strong "societal return on invest-ment" in the activities of the philanthropy-seeking entity.

- Feeling that the value proposition (of what that entity is seeking to achieve) comports with their personal values, including the lessons that life has taught them and, therefore, their self-image and their life's purposes.

- Seeing and being given an opportunity to lend experience, wisdom, or expertise to the shaping of the proposed initiative.

- Understanding with greater and greater certainly where and how specific levels of investment will yield specific institutional or societal returns (this is why it is better to ask donors to give through your organization, not just to it).

- Having a greater willingness to advocate for the cause or purpose, including representing the entity or hosting events on its behalf.

- Seeing how a particular project or initiative will have a particularly significant impact.

- Seeking the counsel and corroborating support for the proposed purposes of that project or initiative from loved ones, friends, respected colleagues, and independent experts

- Moving toward the conclusion that, of all the things they could be doing to make a difference in the world, this project or initiative, at this place and time, under the leadership of this particular dean, is among the most important things—if not the most important thing—they could and should do.

Ask donors to give <u>through</u> your organization, not just <u>to</u> it.

12. *Do* **respond:** Prospects want to feel as if they matter as multi-faceted human beings to the organizations that they support. No one wants to feel as if they are being viewed as a wallet carrier and being sidled up to endlessly and ingratiatingly only to get access to it. The way we can prove to prospects that they matter is to:

   - Genuinely seek their advice and counsel (and show how we have responded to it).

   - Ask them to lend their unique talents to proposed purpose (and respond by showing them how they are making concrete and lasting differences).

   - Encourage them to speak with utter candor about the initiatives we propose and the news we share (and respond appreciatively and without defensiveness).

13. *Do* **master the art and science of vision:** Most certainly, and not long after you begin interacting with prospects and donors, you will be asked, "What's your vision for the school/college?" If you answer with too much specificity too soon, you run the risk of making too many of your listeners feel left out because you haven't conducted a large enough reconnaissance to understand and speak for the hopes of the community. This may lead to foreclosing on possibilities that you have yet

to imagine in your earliest days as a dean.
Conversely, if you answer with too little
specificity or take too long, you will cause
your real and potential community of support
to wonder if you have the ability to lead them
to higher ground. So what's a new dean
supposed to do? What is most important for
you to communicate in your earliest days is
not a mere plan of action, and certainly not a
list of needs; it is a statement of higher and
enduring purposes. The first formulation of a
vision should be about how the entity under
your supervision can better serve. In most
instances, the service imperatives that would
have the greatest resonance with most
prospects and donors, in order of importance,
would be:

- The future of the students in your charge,
  and therefore, the professions, purposes,
  and polities they will serve.

- The generation and dissemination of
  knowledge that will make a difference
  where a difference most needs to be made
  in your field, profession, community, or
  for the sake of humanity itself.

- The application of specific knowledge or
  practice to specific needs and emerging
  opportunities that will result in specific
  improvements to the human condition.

These are the "grabbers" for real and
potential supporters of virtually every area of
academic endeavor. These are the things that
stir the imagination and the soul of
philanthropists.

Deans who articulate higher purposes with authenticity and personal conviction at the outset of their tenures will satisfy current stakeholders and draw forward others with similar intents and purposes. They will buy themselves time to add operational flesh to these thematic bones, and they will use the intervening time to incorporate the voices and talents of those within their organization, and those who might support it, into the whole. Giving the necessary depth of thought to the larger purposes, and the necessary time to listen and incorporate the reactions of others, makes for a sustainable, supportable vision. Some deans might be able to wow their audiences with their thematic vision for the future, but it will come to seem increasingly like wishful, if not delusional, thinking if they cannot explain how they propose to get to the projected promised land or how specific increments of private support will move them inexorably in the intended direction.

Conversely, some deans will be quite adept and convincing on the operational side but will not be able to sustain the morale of those they seek to lead, internally or externally. They risk losing support if they are not able to explain why, how or when greater sacrifices of time, talent, and treasure will result in the achievement of greater purposes. In general, new deans have about a year to get this balance right. While "all eyes turn to the rising sun," after one year, we assume we know the pattern of what is possible and attainable and what is not.

14. ***Do* provide meaning and community:** Generalizations about human nature, or

predictions of human behavior, will invariably crash on the rocks of multi-dimensional realities, but we can learn from what people say they hope to achieve or are looking for in life. When we review various surveys and poll results, "happiness" studies, and other evidence, we see that virtually all of us are in search of two ends, community and meaning. Philanthropy will gravitate disproportionately to those who provide and sustain both.

ENGAGING PROSPECTS WITH THE STRONGEST PHILANTHROPIC PROPENSITY

After you have made your initial rounds of prospect visits and begun to formulate a case for support that both advances the purposes of your school/college and resonates with the interests of those most apt to support you, you will want to begin personalizing the process. This will entail aligning individual prospect interests with specific strategic objectives. While it is typical and prudent to move into this stage with a menu of fundraising objectives (e.g. financial aid, faculty support, programmatic augmentation, capital improvements) based on a strategic assessment of where the college/school can better live out its mission, you cannot succeed by simply shopping that menu around.

Turning that menu into a four-color brochure with the most compelling case written by the best writer you can find does not appreciably strengthen your fundraising hand. The approach is too simplistic and reductive of what should be a rich conversation around greater purposes and possibilities. It says, in effect, to the prospect, "We've got it all figured out; all we need is your money." But if prospects haven't been involved in that strategic assessment, they don't know how you reached your conclusions. If they don't see their point of view, voice, or values reflected in your agenda, they are far less likely to give at the levels at which they are capable.

It is not merely the weight of the evidence you present or the strength of your arguments; it is understanding the resonance and receptivity, or lack thereof, with which your case is met. The larger the amount of support we pursue, the more personal it becomes for the donor. Therefore, the process of major gift fundraising should be built around the exploration of shared purposes and—if and when they are found—the best means by which they can be advanced.

The larger the amount of support we pursue, the more personal it becomes for the donor.

If we remember that the development of a major gift takes **twenty-one months** and takes **nine interactions,** it makes sense to ask what those nine interactions might look like; how each might be best designed and orchestrated; and how each might build on the previous one. While these interactions vary from individual to individual, the enumeration of the following categorical steps seeks to characterize what the progression should look like to help us stay on task during the first three months and use the ensuing eighteen months or more as productively as possible.

Interactions 1-3 | **ENGAGE**
Interaction 4 | **PROPENSITY DETERMINATION**
Interaction 5 | **PROJECT INTRODUCTION**
Interaction 6 | **PROJECT ENGAGEMENT**
Interaction 7 | **PROJECT ALIGNMENT**
Interaction 8 | **WRITTEN PROPOSAL**
Interaction 9 | **CLOSURE**

Interactions 1-3 | ENGAGE

This is what we have discussed up to this point. As a new
dean, you and your development officer (DO) or someone
from advancement has helped you identify your strongest
field of prospects based on their financial capacity and
proven philanthropic propensities. You have engaged
them in a discussion of your larger purposes, asked for
their advice, and listened intently to their responses. This
may involve one to three interactions. The first of these
interactions may have been a visit with them in a place of
their choosing. The second may have been a follow up
visit in which you reported on what you had learned in
ensuing discussions with other critical stakeholders. The
third may have been their attendance at an event on or off
campus in which you spoke with greater clarity about the
emerging direction of the school or college.

In one or more of these interactions, you were likely to
have witnessed a subset of prospects taking a more active
part in the discussion; demonstrating a pronounced
passion on a certain topic or evincing strong convictions
about a certain direction your unit should take; or asking
for more information and, if you're particularly fortunate,
asking how they can help. From those who exhibit these
broad behaviors, you can determine which viewpoints are
most reasonable and constructive, and who possesses
points of view that can be brought into workable
alignment with your own.

Interaction 4 | PROPENSITY DETERMINATION

Working in combination with your DO or advancement
colleague, you need to begin to determine how the broad

interests of your most promising prospects, those that have surfaced in your early engagements, can be converted into deep and specific interests that can be converted into philanthropic support. To better understand a particular prospect's propensity, you need to look at their previous philanthropic giving to your organization, as well as to others.

Is there a pattern to giving? Does this prospect seem to be operating from a decipherable set of philanthropic objectives? Does it reveal his or her values? For instance, a deeper review of a prospect's profile might reveal a pattern of giving primarily to science and technology. In addition, it might reveal the prospect's tendency to support scholarships or student-related activities. Further, you might see in the construction of gifts given previously, a tendency to create scholarships or underwrite programs that allow students to gain more practical experience. Finally, you might pick up on a tendency either to provide a large gift to provide helpful scholarships to a number of students with an emphasis on need or to get behind one stellar student with the scholarship emphasis on academic merit without financial need as an awarding criterion.

Taking the time to understand a particular prospect's propensities, when you can find sufficient evidence of them, will help you introduce a topic that is more likely to be met with more immediate and powerful resonance. Similarly, the absence of this kind of forethought and prior review can lead to unproductive meetings where you and/or your DO may be tossing out ideas that cause promising prospects to conclude that, notwithstanding their initial positive impressions, your agenda is too ill-defined, unconvincing, or too divergent from their purposes.

Interaction 5 | PROJECT INTRODUCTION

If, however, you go well prepared and find something that adds strength to your unit; adds viability to the fulfillment of your school/ college's mission; and resonates with the prospect, you can then begin talking in earnest about what needs to be done and how you intend to go about it.

CASE STUDY: INTERACTION 5

For instance, imagine that your prospect is one who believes in helping students but reveals his belief that scholarships are given too often to those who are determined to be cognitively gifted through overly narrow and statistically insignificant criteria. He further asserts that scholarships should be given in smaller amounts, that the amount of any money given to any student in any given year should constitute no more than one third of his/her total tuition. He states that these gifts should be awarded to students not upon admission, but at the end of the academic year, and only when they have met certain performance criteria, including a minimum GPA and a minimum number of hours worked. He believes the standard approach of giving large scholarships with no stipulation to an arbitrarily narrow band of the cognitively gifted has created a class of entitled elitists who are less likely to be responsible employees, to work effectively in teams, or to be civically engaged and philanthropic. He adds that he has gathered evidence from various universities to suggest an inverse proportion between the size of scholarships and the level of giving to one's alma mater.

In the case study above, you have an example of a prospect offering an individual take on a core need of most institutions: student support. You may or may not find merit in such a suggestion.

Let's say you believe not only that there is merit in his idea, but that it might appeal to others, and would constitute an innovation that would put your school in the middle of an important educational and social experiment. You wonder, if you were able to create a control group of such students, would you be able to compare not only their academic performance over time but the levels of indebtedness with which they graduate; their ability to secure meaningful employment within six weeks of graduation; and their penchant to give back to the area of their major studies.

If so, you've created a powerful philanthropic proposition, a project that aligns prospect purpose with your educational design.

In short, you have found something that you can work on together.

To better appreciate the power of a philanthropic project, imagine a more pedestrian approach, one in which you listen to this same prospect by responding, perhaps too soon, by asking him to fund a standard scholarship while you "explore the feasibility of this other alternative." Your chances of success are very slim. Or what if you accepted much of the criteria he proposed and responded on the spot by asking him to establish a scholarship fund on that basis? You would have been far more likely to achieve success with this approach. But, since you made the ask as soon as possible and did not seek to further engage him in the life of the school or college, you are likely to get less support than this prospect is capable of providing.

If, however, you see the greater potential suggested earlier, you would not ask this prospect to commit to a gift at that moment. You would, instead, request assistance in the design of a larger initiative to test how students might respond to alternate scholarships and to see if an alternate scholarship design produces the desired behaviors over time.

If a prospect is less clear on what he or she may be interested in but has a passion in a particular area—be it the environment, early childhood development, mental health, developing nations, or creating opportunities for ascendant populations—you might try presenting a draft of a white paper that describes an area of scholarly endeavor or a service activity that aligns with one of those passions. A white paper has the same attributes as an effective case for support, but it is still very much a draft; it is, generally, three to five pages in length. It should be presented as an early and incomplete conception of a potential new direction or redirection of an existing effort. The prospect should be asked to review the draft and invited to write his/her suggestions in the margins. When a prospect begins to interact with a draft and to suggest ways of reshaping or refining the core concept, he or she is beginning the process of becoming a shareholder in the enterprise. If you have put a white paper in front of a prospect with real expertise to offer in that area, chances are that some of his or her ideas can be incorporated into the next iteration and to the further shaping of the concept. As this unfolds, an alignment of purpose begins to form.

Interaction 6 | PROJECT ENGAGEMENT

The most effective way of engaging a prospect in a project is to ask for the application of his/her talents and time. The more prospects give of those precious commodities, the more apt they are to invest greater amounts of their treasure. So, let's say the prospect who wants to create a new kind of scholarship has been successful in consulting. You might ask for his expertise in converting strategies into operational practices and efficiencies. That might entail asking him to join you in a discussion with the financial aid director to explore the institution's receptivity to the concept; gauging student reaction through a meeting with students who might fit the bill; developing a set of metrics by which the program could be evaluated; and meeting with the career placement office about the quality and number of internships available to students.

If the project moves out of the conceptual stage, the prospect can be asked to serve as advocate for the project and meet with groups of alumni, business leaders, and potential supporters. It is an extraordinarily good sign when prospects become advocates. We cannot successfully convince others without convincing ourselves, so a commitment to advocacy represents a very positive step toward a deeper financial commitment. All of these suggested actions allow for graceful, productive and progressive interaction with a prospect. They allow him or her to become increasingly familiar with the concept, to better understand what it will take to implement, and to see how private support can be used to make a significant and lasting difference. And, if done well, all of this can be accomplished before asking for a financial commitment. You've used the intervening time to increase the prospect's perception of the value proposition, and to come increasingly to see the project as an extension of his or her values and life purposes.

Interaction 7 | PROJECT ALIGNMENT

If you have taken a prospect through the previous steps of this process, or some reasonable facsimile thereof, you are now ready to seek a formal alignment of purpose. Your chat with the prospect might go something like this:

> "Eric, I appreciate the opportunity to work with you over the past seven months. I've learned a lot in the process and I appreciate the value that you've added to this project. I think we both see what could be done here and why it's so important. I'd appreciate it if we could begin exploring the possibility of your financial support. I'd like you to be the anchor investor. I know of no better way for this to get off to the right start."

In fact, there are all sorts of ways to ask for support before putting a written proposal in front of a prospect. A soft ask is a way of testing the waters with a prospect when one isn't quite certain if it's the right moment. It might go like this,

> "Leslie, I think we've both learned a lot about this project in the last few months. I appreciate how much you've contributed to this initiative and wanted to check in with you to see if we could open up a discussion in the next few weeks, or longer, about the possibility of your financial support."

In that scenario, we check the prospect's receptivity and give her the choice between sooner or later. Checking in from time to time is far better than setting up a formal solicitation and catching a prospect by surprise. A successful solicitation is often a foregone conclusion of a well-executed process.

Interaction 8 | WRITTEN PROPOSAL

If a prospect has signaled his or her receptivity to discussing a gift, the next best step is a face-to-face meeting in which a written proposal is previewed and submitted. Every significant gift request should come in the form of a written proposal. A verbal solicitation without supporting documentation can be taken less seriously or increase the probability of a prospect saying "no." Few people will commit very large sums to vague concepts. The more one gives, the more one needs to justify the amount. A good proposal does just that; it helps establish the legitimacy of the amount being requested and lays out its intended use. It should also explain how the project will be monitored to ensure it fulfills the stated purpose and how the prospect will be kept informed. It should also describe how the prospect will be recognized should s/he make the commitment. Under this recommended scenario, the prospect is encouraged to take the written proposal home, to take the time to digest it, and to share it with loved ones, financial advisors, and others. There's a lot of mythology around verbal solicitation being closed on the spot, but no one brags about those that have resulted in a quick "no" or a much smaller gift than expected. The written proposal is an effective way of avoiding those outcomes by surfacing concerns and objections—those that emerge immediately or after the proposal has been read. The written proposal process often counts as a necessary and effective series of interactions that culminates in large commitments.

Every significant gift request should come in the form of a written proposal. A verbal

solicitation without supporting document-
ation can be taken less seriously or increase
the probability of a prospect saying "no."

Interaction 9 | CLOSURE

In general, the larger the amount requested, the longer it will take to "close" the gift in the form of a written gift agreement. Taking the necessary time to achieve a complete alignment of expectations with a donor creates a happy donor who will generate positive word- of-mouth on your behalf. Further, when the pledge is fulfilled, the donor will be far more likely to give again. Once again, for gifts of any significance (a bar that may vary from institution to institution), it is important to effect a written agreement for several reasons including:

- The formality speaks to the importance of the gift and allows the donor to see the seriousness with which the college/school accepts the respons-ibility.

- It mitigates the possibility of misunderstanding down the road such as a donor claiming the school/college did not deliver on its promise and, when the donor dies, the potential of the gift being challenged by heirs.

- It allows the gift to be more effectively stewarded (a stewardship plan detailing how the gift is to be recognized and how the donor is to be kept informed is a part of many gift agreements).

- It allows for continuity of purpose and the preservation of good relations beyond the tenure of individual deans or development officers.

As you and your DO work your way through these steps, you may be tempted to try to speed up the process or skip a step, but remember you're not just lining up gifts for the use of your school or college. You're trying to build a community of lasting support, one in which donors see how their investments are making a difference and increasingly believe in the agency of your school and, therefore, the reason to give again.

Predictive Indicators of Propensity

Let *propensity* drive solicitation. Your DO should not suggest that every prospect should be solicited at the level of his or her capacity ranking. A seasoned DO should advise soliciting only after making sure that the prospect in question has a strong propensity ranking and is evincing a very strong interest in a particular project.

The circumstances most predictive of the giving a significant portion of one's wealth include:

- Long and deep engagement with the school/ college including significant volunteer stints, often including board leadership.

- Ten or more years of previous giving.

- Multiple family connections to the school (including representatives of multiple generations, multiple siblings, and/or one or more children having attended).

- Recent and significant interactions with the school.

- An almost unshakeable sense on the donor's part that his or her personal, professional, and/or spiritual interests can be best realized by working with and through the school.

When we see these factors in a prospect's profile, we can assign a much higher "propensity" ranking to the prospect. That ranking is far more revealing and predictive than the formulaic wealth ranking. Wealth rankings are important because 24% of Americans control 80% of the total wealth, but high net worth, in and of itself, is not predictive of philanthropic behavior, much less remarkable acts of generosity.

In some circumstances, where strong relationships have been built over time, and when a school puts forward a project or initiative that deeply resonates with a donor's passion, a donor might give far more than five percent of his or her net worth. In quite a few instances, long-term alignment of purposes has led donors to leave most or all of their estates to certain schools.

The Most Important Indicator

The single best indicator of what a person might give next is what they gave last to yours or any other philanthropy-seeking organization.

Perceptions of one's net worth, liquidity, security, and philanthropic wherewithal vary wildly and can be rooted far more deeply in emotion than in fact. Those who are philanthropic rarely begin giving at the levels at which development operations rate them. More often than not, they begin giving at modest levels. Then, when they seek the impact of their giving and realize that their giving had not adversely affected their annual budget or sense of long-term security, they give more.

In fact, most donors "stair step" their way up to higher levels of gift commitments over time—rather than suddenly leap up to much higher amounts.

AN EXAMPLE

So, if you find yourself in a situation where you hope to secure a $1 million gift to launch a major initiative and find there are two prospects ranked with that capacity, look a little deeper.

Perhaps Prospect A has a gift capacity ranking of $5 million but has never given more than $100,000 to any organization.

Prospect B has a ranking of $2 million and has given as much as $750,000.

Go with Prospect B.

GOOD DEVELOPMENT OFFICERS

Finally, in the rank ordering of prospects or the formulation of engagement strategies for each donor, your DO should be able to demonstrate repeatedly how he or she brings good judgment to bear.

Good DOs don't treat their deans like bait, dangling them in front of questionable prospects to see if "something might happen." Skilled development professionals pore over research and prospect profiles and personally engage a large field of prospects before bringing any of them to the dean's attention.

And when a recommendation is made, it includes suggestions as to when and where the meeting should occur, what makes this particular prospect tick, where this particular prospect is in regards to length and level of engagement, and what you might do at the next meeting to further align purposes.

Smart, secure DOs know when to accompany you on prospect calls and when to operate behind the scenes, as well as how to best complement your calls by visiting the prospect in advance, after the fact, or both.

WORKING WITH YOUR PRESIDENT

Many presidents delegate significant authority for the day-to-day running of the academic enterprise to their provosts; this allows them to fulfill their external responsibilities, the most time consuming of which is fundraising. Chances are that you are reporting to a provost or chief academic officer but may find yourself working directly or indirectly with the president on fundraising opportunities.

Presidents' ability to secure private support has become an increasingly important element of their annual evaluation, both by the formal evaluations done by those that they report to and the ongoing evaluation of the stakeholders in the institutions they represent. Given those pressures and expectations, it should not be a surprise to see presidents seeking to mobilize all available assets, including all available prospects, to achieve greater fundraising results. And it is reasonable for a president to assert that prospects, like all other institutional resources, must be managed and marshaled to achieve the highest institutional purposes.

At the same time, evaluators and stakeholders expect deans to be more active and successful fundraisers. Deans will naturally seek to optimize the philanthropic potential of their most prominent prospects. When they do, they may be told by central advancement that some or even many of those prospects have been claimed by the president. If that is the case at your institution, you may be advised not to contact those prospects, to contact them only after permission has been given, and/or to let central advancement know when you are about to contact them and to file a "contact report" after the fact. If all of this seems to be a case of too much responsibility and too little authority, it is important to remember that advancement is not a zero-sum game.

Successful presidents raise confidence in their institution, thereby increasing its ability to compete for even higher levels of support.

If you have an active, effective fundraising president you stand to gain far more than you will lose. Successful presidents raise confidence in their institution thereby increasing its ability to compete for even higher levels of support. Further, presidents work with prospects that have the greatest capacity to give, period. If those prospects have a deep interest in one of more of the disciplines in your college, a smart president will seek to leverage, not divert, that interest. The president's attention to such prospects, in most instances, will result in a higher likelihood of their giving, or giving more, than if you were approaching them by yourself.

Therefore, you would be wise to effect or strengthen the collaboration with the president and his/her office. You can do this by:

- Expressing your support of the president's priorities up the academic chain-of-command and in all public venues.

- Providing examples of how the president's priorities can be more fully realized, or examples of how they are already yielding specific successes, in your unit.

- Demonstrating your willingness to represent your institution as a whole when you are on the road or in public settings.

- Being open and accountable to central prospect management systems.

- Keeping the inevitable stresses and strains in the collaborative framework completely "in the family."

A KEY RESOURCE

Your DO—or your president—may be interested in the book *Fundraising for Presidents*, where I outline and provide stirring examples of what an active, effective fundraising president looks like, and how they can partner most effectively with others involved in fundraising.

You can order copies of that book here:

https://www.academicimpressions.com/product/fundraising-presidents-guide/

WORKING WITH CENTRAL ADVANCEMENT

If your experience is like that of many deans at other institutions of higher learning, you will encounter some occasional frustrations in working with the central development operation or with the president's office. In one sense, it is all but inevitable; prospects are resources, and the allocation of any resource across a landscape of needs or among competing claimants will never satisfy everyone.

The Importance of Getting Informed

It will be important for you to understand the practices and policies at your institution that govern the identification, allocation, and tracking of prospects. You might find yourself in an environment where you have tremendous leeway in those areas, or perhaps you are in an environment where there simply are no systems in place to govern those practices (the latter is highly unlikely). Conversely, there are some environments that are so centralized that deans are precluded from having any contact with any prospects. In all likelihood, you have some responsibility for fundraising. The question is how much responsibility and if you have a commensurate amount of authority to act effectively on it.

You have, no doubt, inherited a subset of prospects, including virtually all of your living graduates. The only exceptions might be those prospects and donors who have been deemed worthy of the president's attention. That does not mean necessarily that these prospects are no longer yours but that they are of such prominence that the president can't afford to ignore them. Their loyalties may remain with your school/college; if so, you should work closely with central development and the president's office rather than try to wrest them away. Presidential attention to your prospects will work more often in your favor than not.

Presidential attention to your prospects will work more often in your favor than not.

The other exception may be when your graduates have gravitated to other interests. A graduate of an engineering school, for example, may have developed a passion for music and aligned herself with the center for performing arts on campus. Or an English major may have become deeply committed to environmental sciences. If your university is to optimize the potential of all the prospects at its disposal, it will allow each to gravitate to areas that they deem of being most worthy of their philanthropic support. Most deans in most high functioning systems understand the power of letting donors decide what they want to give to, within reason, and don't seek to block their migration. In that sense, "the donor decides" is a core tenet of prospect allocation in sophisticated and successful fundraising cultures. They understand that no single entity can "own" a prospect but that the interests of the whole institution are served when all internal stakeholders collaborate to allow prospects to seek and express their unique philanthropic values.

Some deans, believing that central development and/or the president's office have and will continue to poach their best prospects, stop registering their prospect interactions with the central development's tracking systems. In a "donor decides" environment, that practice can backfire because a prospect, in the face of competing claims or needs, will be allocated to those who can show that they have had the greatest, most significant, and recent interaction with him or her. If you haven't recorded your interactions and shared them with central development, they cannot protect your claims.

So, in working with a central advancement office, it is important to understand the means by which prospects are allocated to units and to know how to manage them so that they remain your resources. The longer you maintain a relationship with prospects, the greater the probability of their giving your school/college greater amounts of support and, ultimately, a larger portion of their estate. In most cases, the relationship that your best donors will enjoy with your school or college will exceed your tenure. Treat your eventual successor as you would have had your predecessor treat you: leave full and accurate records of prospect and donor relationships so they can be managed to the greatest effect over time.

> *Treat your eventual successor as you would have had your predecessor treat you: leave full and accurate records of prospect and donor relationships so they can be managed to the greatest effect over time.*

Prospects are only as good as the time and attention you afford them. No dean can ignore his or her prospects while insisting that others keep their hands off. In such cases, central development has every right to insist that any attention paid to prospects, by anyone at the university, is better than none; this may result in your prospects being reassigned to someone who will be more attentive to them.

For these reasons, many central advancement operations will make a preliminary assignment of prospects based on certain assumptions—such as deans having the first claim on their graduates. However, to encourage prospect interaction, and to give prospects the opportunity to gravitate toward areas of greatest interest, their policies will allow for "open cultivation," meaning any university representative can invite any prospect to any event or engage them in conversation as long as it does not, in any way, touch on the need for private support. If any institutional representative does want to broach the subject of private support, or even the need for additional resources to pursue an opportunity, he or she, in these systems, must file an "intent to solicit" with central development. That "intent" is then posted for two or three days to allow others to contest it, should they feel they have had more relevant and recent contact with that prospect. If the "intent" is uncontested, the filer is given a limited amount of time, generally three to six months, to secure support from the assigned prospect. If the filer of the claim is not successful, the prospect is returned to open cultivation.

The Importance of a Two-Way Partnership

A dean's relationship to central advancement should not be one- sided. Yes, the management of prospects should be a central function, but it should be done in an open, collaborative and coordinated manner. Vice presidents for advancement will lose credibility and sacrifice optimal results if they fail to communicate with deans and put more emphasis on the exertion of control than on demonstrable competence and service. The best advancement leaders don't just insist that everyone must work through the system; they demonstrate how everyone's interests are best served by working together. In addition, astute advancement leaders place a significant and ongoing emphasis on new prospect discovery. Deans who are getting a steady supply of new prospects are far less likely to clamor for access to prospects already under management. The perception of scarcity, as is true with all resources, can lead to intense infighting.

A Word of Caution: If Your Unit is Raising Less Money

While central advancement will always seek to ensure that the best prospects are managed for the greatest institutional gain, which is usually defined by the president's priorities, it is important to remember that it does not raise money for itself. Advancement leaders want to raise as much as possible; in which unit it lands matters little. Deans who act on the suspicion that advancement is "playing favorites" or doing more for other units by clamoring or griping incessantly, therefore, are not likely to help their cause.

While playing the squeaky wheel may be effective on occasion in fighting internal budgeting battles, this method is never effective in influencing philanthropic decisions. Donors don't give so that everyone will have a fair share; they give to people and programs that they believe have the greatest probability of producing a greater good in an area that they care most deeply about. Advancement officers are agnostic when it comes to internal politics; they seek to match institutional strengths with prospects' interests.

> **Advancement officers are agnostic when it comes to internal politics; they seek to match institutional strengths with prospects' interests.**

If your unit is raising less money than others, it is less likely that advancement has done you wrong, and more likely that:

- The philanthropic market has greater interest in other areas (e.g. medicine will invariably attract more private support than literature).

- Too much emphasis has been placed on asking, and too little on building a community of purpose that will be receptive to the request (imagine, for instance, a minister going door- to-door holding out a collection basket to those who have never met him or know nothing about his faith vs. passing the basket among a congregation that feels consistently uplifted by its faith and personally well-served by a selfless, hardworking, solicitous minister).

- You need to develop a more compelling case for support (one that speaks in convincing and practical terms about how prospects can give through your school/college to create a better world).

- You need to work on improving, or find someone who complements, your communication ability and relationship- building skills.

To the last point, remember philanthropy is about the search for better ways and promised lands. Philanthropy gravitates to optimists with compelling plans. You can't just want more for yourself or your unit; you must see a way of better serving a higher purpose through the auspices of your college/school, and you must be able to describe where and how specific amounts, in part and in whole, will yield higher thresholds of achievement.

New deans should seek out their vice president for advancement and ask his or her advice on how their unit can better position itself for increased levels of private support and how they can be as effective as possible, including what texts they may read, successful deans they may learn from, and conferences that would be most worth their while.

WORKING WITH ALUMNI RELATIONS: YOUR ENTIRE SCHOOL'S RESPONSIBILITY

Those who are most apt to be your most loyal supporters and, therefore, the greatest source of major and estate gifts, are your grateful beneficiaries, your alumni.

Yet, this most probable source of support is in the steepest decline.

This is due to a combination of factors, According to research done by the Engagement Strategies Group, one of these factors is the conviction that "my alma mater does little to connect with me beyond asking for money." This sentiment is more likely to be expressed by alumni whose alma maters have tightly controlled access to them, while having too few advancement staff to maintain consistent contact with them. Alumni and others do not want their connections to their alma mater to be restricted to advancement staff who, by definition, manage alumni relations only toward one end. They are also not interested in only connecting with university representatives who see alumni only as a means of financial support, who can be implored for money at every opportunity. This tendency has contributed to a steady decline in the percentage of alumni participation and, therefore, a decline in the probability of future major gifts and estate commitments. For too long, we have celebrated increasing amounts of private support, but the "dollars up" has been, in the vast majority of cases, at the cost of "donors down." The steady loss of donors over the past few decades has left many schools, colleges, and universities seriously attenuated if not broken "pipelines" of private support.

Enlightened deans or, in some cases, deans with no other choice, will focus the preponderance of their efforts on building community with their alumni and other prospects. This must be done with authenticity, by believing and convincing them that they are valued for who they are and what they have accomplished.

You can achieve this by:

- Acknowledging and celebrating the good that your alumni have done with their lives, including volunteer service to others.

- Creating a listening environment in which their opinions are being sought on all important matters and through a variety of means including your personal elicitations, focus groups, and telephonic and electronic surveys.

- Asking alumni still working in the fields represented by your college or school to be your strategic scouts, to telegraph back where those fields are changing, or facing new realities and emerging opportunities, so that you can make the necessary adjustments and give your students a jump on the future.

- Making it known that you are constantly searching for alumni talents and experience that can be used to enhance your curricular offerings, create internships and other extra- curricular opportunities. Tell alumni that these offerings and internships will give students a chance to apply their learning and learn by doing, contain costs and thereby enhance value, boost morale and impart a greater sense of meaning, and allow your graduates to be more employable or lead more satisfying lives.

- Convening meetings and discussions around matters of great import to your alumni and their families that intersect with the expertise of your faculty. These issues may include elementary or high school reform or coping with family members afflicted with a disease—particularly those with growing prevalence (e.g. autism and Alzheimer's).

- Leveraging faculty relationships with alumni:

  o Informal or formal advisory boards.

  o Reporting/informing advancement colleagues on any classroom visits.

Young alumni, particularly those saddled with tuition-related debt, might be particularly sensitive to appeals for "giving back." They are apt to feel as if they already are by repaying their student loans, even as they seek more meaningful employment. If young alumni fall away because of the one-dimensionality of your offerings, they will be harder and harder to get back as time elapses. And when their means increase, in some cases quite drama-tically, it will be very difficult to convince them that you had their best interests at heart all along.

We know a lot about alumni who give and about institutions that inspire the highest levels of their sustained support. We know that people give when they feel a valued part of an important community of purpose. Anything you can do to create that sense of community will serve your purposes well, and that of your school or college long after your tenure.

We can't create community by merely asking for support, but we can be far more successful in securing support from those who feel they are a part of a reciprocating community.

When fundraising becomes too linear and short-term, when every act of outreach appears to be a direct or lightly veiled attempt to secure more support, that sense of community is damaged and the prospects of fundraising are diminished. Therein lies the paradox: the more you convert all purposes to fundraising, the less likely you are to sustain or grow support over time. Yet, the more you subordinate the immediate need for support to the greater imperative of creating "mattering members" of your community, the more you raise.

Anything less than a 9:1 ratio of non-fundraising to fundraising interactions between a school and its alumni is likely to perpetuate the alumni feeling that you only want their money.

According to an analysis reported in CASE Currents, anything less than a 9:1 ratio of non-fundraising to fundraising interactions between a school and its alumni is likely to perpetuate the alumni feeling that you only want their money. Yet, when one looks at where money is invested in most advancement operations, far more is allocated to short-term fundraising than to alumni communications or alumni relations. Anything you can do to rebalance that equation and to show a greater and more genuine interest in your alumni will pay a significant and long-term dividend to your college.

Finally, remember that alumni participation is an out-growth of the student experience. The making or unmaking of an active, supportive alumnus can be traced back to the first semester of the freshman year. If a new student suffers an emotional trauma, or feels neglected or unguided at critical moments, he or she is not likely to want to revisit those memories later in life. Conversely, the most loyal of alumni maintain a lifelong gratitude for professors who not only taught their subject material, but took the time to offer encouragement, support, and guidance. Alumni of colleges and universities that enjoy the highest levels of loyal support believe strongly that the value of their degree over time greatly exceeded the cost. They do not attribute that value to subject matter taught during their student experience, but to the personal encouragement afforded and the feeling that they are a vital part of an important, purposeful community.

MANAGING PROSPECT PORTFOLIOS

Achieving and sustaining fundraising success requires one to find the balance point between disparate tensions—patient persistence, certain but adaptive direction setting, a singular but integrative vision, a willingness to negotiate but only up to a certain point, and flexible organization. When working with a group of individual prospects, you cannot expect to drive the agenda entirely to his or her liking or timetable. Nor can you expect to merely execute a series of "moves" and expect your prospects to acquiesce accordingly. The fundraising equivalent to Napoleon's assertion that "no battle plan survives the first engagement with the enemy" is "no series of pre-conceived moves survives the first interactions with prospects." Even under the best of circumstances, the securing of a major gift can entail not only a 21-month period and nine interactions; it may also require you to make 100 subtle adjustments along the way. That is why the overall management of large fields of prospects requires a high degree of organization and discipline.

That discipline begins with the formulation of a prospect list and the criteria applied so that it may be ranked. A dean working with a single DO would be wise to think about creating a portfolio of no more than 120 prospects in four tiers of 30. The top 30 should be thought of as your most promising prospects (MPPs). They should constitute those prospects with the highest combined capacity and propensity scores (see Appendix A). Propensity scores should be based on the strength of the prospect's record of giving, especially to your organization or to a similar cause or purpose. Those in the first tier should also be the most recently engaged. Even those with the highest combined ratings should not be at the top of your list if they have not been seen in months. If you have not dated a romantic partner in months, you would not expect to talk about making a deep commitment on the next date. You would first see if you could get the date, then spend more time with him/her until there was evidence of increasingly shared interests. The same is true of prospect management. If none of your MPPs have been met with in months, you will have to scale back your short-term fundraising expectations and commit yourself to six months of intensive and considerate interaction with the top 30.

The amount of time you must be prepared to spend on engaging prospects depends on the state of the relationships you have inherited and the degree of difference you want to make. If the state of your prospect relationships is relatively weak and your ambitions are high, you should be prepared to spend half your time working with prospects. If you have inherited a strong set of relationships or your ambitions are more modest or focused, you might find yourself allocating a third of your time to these tasks. Anything significantly below or above that range is unrealistic or unsustainable.

The First Tier in Your Portfolio

As a general rule of thumb, you should try to allocate fifty percent of your external activities to your top 30, striving for personal, productive, and progressive interaction with each prospect every four to six weeks. If you let two more months elapse between substantive interactions with your top 30, you will need to reorganize your calendar or challenge your commitment to this purpose. Given the increased number and size of fundraising organizations, and the growing sophistication of their prospect identification and predictive analytical methodology, it is highly unlikely that any of your top 30 have not been pursued or engaged by at least six other philanthropy-seeking entities. To be as successful as possible, you must assume that others have been courting your top prospects and you should be willing to stay on task and message. You don't have to fawn, humor, or ingratiate but you do need to be present, positive, and precise throughout the process of aligning purposes with your most likely sources of support.

Allocating External Activities

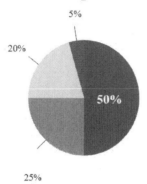

✎ **50% of your external activities should be allocated to your first tier**

✎ 25% allocated to second tier

✎ 20% allocated to third tier

✎ 5% allocated to new prospects

The most important criterion for determining whether a prospect is assigned to the top tier is a high probability that they will commit to a gift in the next six to twelve months. This would suggest that they have years of giving to their school/college or a long record of philanthropy, that you have had multiple and recent interactions, that you appear to have found an area or initiative of great interest to them, and that they seem ready for more explicit conversations about how it can be advanced.

In orchestrating a high degree of steady and substantive engagement, you can call upon many well-established methods, including:

- Setting up one-on-one meetings in which you seek the opinions and/or expertise of the prospect or discuss how his/her talents might apply to the advancement of your mission.

- Inviting prospects to intimate events, including salon events or Jeffersonian dinners, in which you engage twelve to twenty top prospects, preferably around a single table in a conducive setting, in a discussion around a strategic objective.

- Requesting and responding to feedback on white papers that preview early stage initiatives.

- Providing a "front row" or "green room" meeting with an impressive speaker before he/she presents at one of your most interesting events.

- Offering a representational or ceremonial role (hosting events, introducing speakers, speaking on your behalf at major functions on or off campus).

- Requesting that prospects serve in a formal-advisory or problem-solving capacity (advisory board, kitchen cabinet, task force).

Remember, volunteers give ten times as much over the course of their lives than non-volunteer donors. As early as 1989, Peter Drucker said: "More and more volunteers are educated people in managerial or professional jobs.... These people are not satisfied with being helpers. They are knowledge workers in the jobs in which they earn their living, and they want to be knowledge workers in the jobs in which they contribute to society.... If nonprofit organizations want to attract and hold them, they have to put their competence and knowledge to work, they have to offer meaningful achievement." That will be particularly true for your top tier prospects.

The Second Tier in Your Portfolio

Allocating External Activities

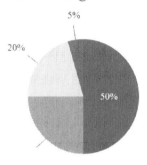

- ✗ 50% of your external activities should be allocated to your first tier
- **✗ 25% allocated to second tier**
- ✗ 20% allocated to third tier
- ✗ 5% allocated to new prospects

Approximately another twenty-five percent of your time should be spent with your second tier of prospects, and many of the aforementioned methods can be employed, albeit with slightly less personal and less frequent interactions. If you have assigned prospects to this tier, it would suggest that more time should be spent in the earlier stages of the fundraising cycle, including exploring areas of potential interests but not in an overt fundraising context. You should seek to interact with these prospects every eight to ten weeks.

The Third Tier in Your Portfolio

Allocating External Activities

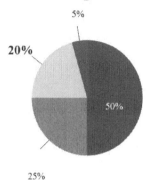

- 50% of your external activities should be allocated to your first tier
- 25% allocated to second tier
- **20% allocated to third tier**
- 5% allocated to new prospects

For those in your third tier, you should allocate approximately 20% of your time. Prospects assigned to this tier might be newly qualified or engaged. Your best approach will be to interview them, asking about the issues they care most about or their most rewarding volunteer activities, all the while listening for areas of mutual interest or common cause.

Another group that belongs in this tier is the donor who has given for many years but at a fairly modest amount. They are important in their own right because of their loyalty and because, as a group, they constitute the "bond portion" of your private support, the predictable portion of your annual private support. Further, they are the most likely to give your college a significant portion of their estate (and don't forget to be attentive to faculty and staff who fall into this category).

Also in this category would be those who have already made estate commitments to you. Most of these commitments will be revocable, so it's wise not to take them for granted and to hope, with your additional efforts, that they might increase the portion assigned to your school/college. You should try to personally interact with these donors, on a one-to-one basis or in small groups, once a quarter.

The Last Tier in Your Portfolio

Allocating External Activities

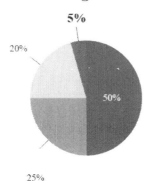

- 50% of your external activities should be allocated to your first tier
- 25% allocated to second tier
- 20% allocated to third tier
- **5% allocated to new prospects**

In the last tier, your prospects should be those who are of great promise but just recently identified. Knowing that they are just entering a philanthropic cycle, you will want to make them feel welcomed into your community and valued for their intelligence, expertise, and experience. You will not want to broach fundraising objectives, except as a part of your overall strategic objectives, for ten to twelve months and you might think about touching base with them two or three times in that period.

Without a degree of discipline, your best intentions to engage and interact with your most promising prospects can easily be crushed by the tyranny of the urgent. These urgent situations may include a welter of campus meetings, personnel issues, faculty needs and concerns, student-related issues, and budgetary dilemmas, all of which emerge and subside with utter unpredictability.

How Large Should Your Portfolio Be?

Further, you will discover that the only truly manageable portfolios are those that contain 120 prospects or fewer. Anything larger than that makes it difficult to maintain the exquisite attention that one most pay to the most promising prospects. Large portfolios also hamper the qualitative review of those being managed by one or more DOs.

> *The only truly manageable portfolios are those that contain 120 prospects or fewer.*

Advancement operations that assign larger portfolios to their DOs and hold them to simplistic metrics (e.g. dollars raised per annum, number of prospect contacted, etc.) come to realize that people will do exactly what you expect. If you hold development officers to a per annum dollar goal they will want large portfolios to increase the chances of meeting that goal. Keep in mind they won't be able to pay proper attention to most of their prospects but those who are innately philanthropic tend to give whether they are sought out or not.

If a large portfolio of prospects is put together with any care, it will contain a large number of such prospects. The more such prospects DOs have in their portfolios, the higher the probability they will meet their requisite dollar goal. But, that doesn't mean that the prospects in those portfolios will engage in a substantive way as we have suggested earlier. That, in turn, means that your school/college will not optimize their full philanthropic potential and increases the likelihood that another organization will capture a larger share of it. Or, if you hold your DOs to a requisite number of prospect contacts, you will discover that those goals are invariably met. But if you look closer, you will see in some cases that some of those contacts consisted of inconsequential encounters, like the exchange of pleasantries at campus events. The key phrase in that sentence is "if you look closer." High achieving advancement cultures place more emphasis on quality than quantity, on developing sustained sources of support not just the securing of gifts, and on building larger and stronger communities of purpose over time.

Finally, the segmenting of prospects into tiers allows you to place disproportionate emphasis on your most promising prospects, which increases your chances of both optimizing their greater potential and securing their commitments within the year. Upon securing those commitments, you can then turn the greater measure of your time to the next most promising group and do the same. This creates more constant upward movement in your portfolios, which results in the more systematic closure of more and larger gift commitments. Without this segmented approach, and absent substantive, project-oriented engagement, one sees prospects stuck in the Hansel and Gretel deep dark woods of "cultivation" for eons. Indeed, it is such a forest of ill-definition, wishful thinking, and obscure practice, that many a prospect has been led into it and few donors have emerged from it.

SUSTAINING THE QUALITY OF YOUR DONOR RELATIONSHIPS

If you are to be as successful as possible in capturing the attention of new prospects, raising the philanthropic sights of existing ones, and enhancing the credibility of, and appreciation for, your school/ college, you will have to do more than manage your prospects. You will have to manage the stream of communication going to and coming back from them. The larger your school/college, the greater this challenge because you will have more people representing you (assistant deans, faculty, multiple advancement staff, etc.) in the field and interacting with your prospects and key constituents. If those represent-atives are not working from a common base of information, or not required to record their interactions with key prospects, you increase the chances of diluting the impact on those whose time, talent, and treasure you are working so hard to secure.

To make this point more vividly, imagine if:

- Some development representatives, including those working for you or supporting your efforts in central development, were describing your purposes and strategic objectives in inaccurate or ineffective ways.

FUNDRAISING FOR DEANS: A GUIDE

- A highly promising prospect heard about one of your initiatives, became intrigued by it, and asked a DO for more information about it, but had to wait weeks and weeks to hear back.

- An important prospect said she was interested in supporting your school/college but was in the middle of a business transition or personal crisis and asked to not be contacted by the college for the next six months, only to receive multiple calls days after making that request.

- A false and potentially damaging rumor began circulating among your prospects and alumni, but you did not hear about it until it had become widespread and far more difficult to manage.

The first two instances underscore the importance of managing the consistency, quality, and timeliness of information going out. The best way to address that issue is to create an intranet function or virtual repository for information that is critical to your fundraising efforts. That might include a fact sheet, a compilation of your most distinctive features and/or accomplishments, answers to FAQs about your school/college, white papers describing all early stage initiatives, your bio, and a slate of your upcoming events. The more time you give to building this virtual file cabinet and the more you fill it with accurate, relevant, compelling, and timely information, the more consistently you can respond to prospects' questions, needs, and concerns, and the more you can accelerate major gift negotiations.

The second two instances speak to the need for managing information coming back into your organization. It is imperative that all those representing your interests and those of your school/ college be required to file contact reports after interacting with your prospects; it is important for you do so, too. All too often, this imperative is misinterpreted at a function of the advancement office's need to control; in fact, it is essential to your school/college's ability to manage relationships over time in the most adroit and sensitive manner possible. If you inherited little of this from your predecessor, make it a hallmark of your tenure to do better by your successor, so he or she can build on your efforts and create an even broader and deeper of community of purpose.

Managing Prospect Information

What sort of information might you need at your fingertips to ensure that you, personally, best represent the school/college and most effectively interact with your key constituents? Some organizations are given to building overly extensive and detailed profiles on their donors and prospects. In such cases, it can be difficult to glean what is most important.

Consider your top prospect, Sally Smith. If you're meeting Sally for the first time, what information is most important for you? You likely want to know:

- Sally's occupation or her life work.

- Her history of giving time, talent, and treasure to your school/college or to the larger institution of which you may be a part.

In other words, donors would hope you know who they are and what they have done for you. Yes, it is important to show your awareness and appreciation of the financial support they have given. You don't have to mention the exact number of cumulative giving, but mentioning the span of time in which they have been giving would be appropriate and appreciated. However, if that is the only part of their record that you cite, it might seem to indicate that it is the only part of the relationship that you care about. If you are expressing gratitude for one's record of service, be sure to cite all the dimensions of it, when applicable, including volunteer work, faithful attendance at important events, taking on leadership roles, and the lending of expertise. The only personal information the donor might expect you to be aware of is which other family members have attended your school/college, particularly children. Demonstrating too much knowledge, let's say by listing off details of family histories, business transactions, or financial records might prove unsettling and make the donor feel as if you've conducted some sort of investigation.

What is most important to deduce from what one does for a living or their life's work, and their giving records, is their value system. What are they trying to do with their life? What passions animate them? What issues most concern them? What has life taught them and how might they want to employ philanthropy to share the meaning of their lives with others? If your records do not reveal these propensities, it would be wise to listen for them in your initial meetings and to make sure that your insights on these matters are entered into the prospect's records. In fact, nothing will prove more important as you seek to frame engagement strategies and achieve an alignment of purpose. And nothing is more important to leave to those who will manage those relationships in future, whether it is your successor or other development officers. The key questions in assessing a prospect's philanthropic potential are:

- What is their record of giving time, talent, and treasure (if not to us than to any organization)?

- How generous are they within their financial means?

- Is there a pattern to their giving that reveals a particular passion or strong sense of purpose? If so, from what personal experiences did it arise?

Seeking out and trying to understand donors' purposes while working to align your aspirations with them is at the heart of sophisticated and successful fundraising.

In imagining, managing, staging, or evaluating events that your school/college might host on or off campus, look for and seek to strengthen the correlation between event attendance and major gift prospect interaction. In too many instances, the correlation is very weak. In other words, you're expending a lot of energy and expense on events that are not drawing out and more substantively engaging your most promising prospects. By simply asking for this analysis, you will help your advancement operation think more strategically. If you review this data and see too few of your top prospects in attendance and/or a relatively small cohort of the "same people" are attending all of your events, and that the majority of those attendees are not giving more time, talent, or treasure as a result of repeated attendance, you need to engage in a fundamental rethinking and retooling of your event schedule. In particular, you will need to ask:

- What can we do to get more of our most promising prospects (MPPs) to our best events? Do we need to invite them in a more personal way? Do we need to give them a more important role (emcee, host, discussion leader, etc.)?

- Do we need to redesign our events so that they have greater appeal or more directly call up on the expertise or passions of our MPPs? Are our events sufficiently substantive to attract the interests of very busy people?

- Do we need to be more imaginative in the way or where we stage our events? Have they become stale, predictable and inconsequential?

- If we are able to get our MPPs to an event, how will it strengthen their understanding of what we are trying to achieve? How will it help us better understand what they are trying to achieve?

- Are we trying to stage so many events that we are not able to do justice to any of them? Would it be wiser to stage fewer events to achieve more strategic attendance and greater impact?

When preparing to attend an event staged by your school or college, ask for a list of RSVPs with MPPs highlighted. If some MPPs are in attendance and you have not met them before, take the time to review their profiles with an eye toward their record of contributions and philanthropic propensities. Take advantage of the occasion to establish a rapport with them, not by trying to impress them with what you or the school/college are doing but how you might better learn from their experience (including their previous interactions with your school/college) and expertise.

You certainly do not want any of your MPPs leaving one of your events feeling slighted, undervalued or as if their attendance did not matter. This is where an effective partnership with your DO can pay off. You should meet in advance, determine with whom your time is best spent, and work out a plan to strategically navigate the room. If, for instance, one attendee dominates your time, it is helpful for your DO to intercept the conversation and explain that another person has requested your attention. That will allow you to politely break off and move on. No, you don't want to be so keen on getting to a few MPPs that you blow by other attendees or fail to keep eye contact with them as you search the room. You can be both a gracious host to the many and strategically attentive to a few. Remember, loyal donors and those who are generous within their means should always be considered MPPs.

APPENDICES

Appendix A: Campaigns—A Primer

Feasibility: Past, Present, and Future

Feasibility studies have been a fixture of campaign planning for some time. In general, they entail testing the feasibility of raising a particular amount of money in a particular period of time. This is done by a broad assessment of an institution's previous fundraising patterns, a look at the depth and breadth of its current prospect pool, and the application of "predictive analytics" projecting future fundraising potential. Perhaps the most important process is a series of private, confidential, individual interviews in which MPPs (particular that 10-20 percent who has the capacity to give 80-90 percent of the campaign total) are asked to react to the institution's initial case for support and the strategic plan on which it is based. During these interviews, they reveal their level of confidence in the institution's leadership, advancement office, and capability to stage and sustain a successful fund drive. Fundraising consultants, who can be seen by MPPs as objective and independent of an institution's politics, have the best chance of securing the most candid and insightful testimony. They protect the confidentiality of the MPPs by compiling and reporting their testimony without attributing any single quotation to any single prospect. And the "read" they provide on MPPs' perceptions of an institution and level of receptivity to a future fundraising request can be invaluable. Often, they reveal considerable disparities between the aspirations of an institution and the enthusiasm of its most likely sources of support. A well-constructed feasibility interview should reveal the MPPs relative level of receptivity to an institution's requests.

Some prospects, for instance, can respond very positively to every question, but when asked, "Where would you place this institution in your overall priorities," will say "fifth," "sixth" or lower. This is sobering news for an institution that has come to believe they are that prospect's highest priority. Yet, any disparity between institutional aspirations and prospects' receptivity that can be detected before solicitation gives that institution the opportunity to adjust and correct.

Since it is rare for any single prospect or donor to support only one organization, many institutions have the same names on the top of their prospect pyramids. Remembering this fact will help you remember why it is important to stay on task and to maintain a schedule of regular and substantive interactions with yours. Further, the testimony of many top prospects of many institutions can be compared to reveal the emerging patterns. In recent years, many remarkably generous philanthropists have stressed the need for greater institutional accountability and to project and demonstrate more clearly the impact of their individual giving and private support in general. Some fear that institutions are asking for private support to avoid, not empower, strategic decision-making. They wonder if institutions have done enough to avoid waste, eliminate duplication, and create greater economies of scale to ensure that private support can truly be "the margin of excellence." They want to see less rhetoric in institutional cases and more evidence of strategic choice making. They want institutions of higher learning to rethink the economic models of the past fifty years and to be more innovative about enhancing quality while containing costs. Increasingly, they question the costs, utility and long-term flexibility of new buildings. Simply being mindful of these growing concerns will help you in your early interactions with seasoned philanthropists. Any commitment you make to more courageous, selective decision- making, to placing more emphasis on service to society over individual or institutional, or to the more careful definition of where private support can make a measurable difference will be met with appreciation and encouragement.

Yet, as valuable as a feasibility study may be, too many institutions have relied too heavily on them in their most traditional form. Feasibility studies are valuable because they are a means of listening to and incorporating the feedback of key constituents to achieve a greater alignment of purposes. Those ends can be achieved in many other ways and often with better long-term results. Engaging MPPs and other key constituents in the early stages of strategic planning, for instance, could yield invaluable insight from those working in the disciplines your school/college represents. They could tell you how those fields are shifting and how your curriculum will have to adapt to keep up and to continue to provide opportunities for future graduates. You can deploy current students to interview unengaged alumni about their animating passions so that you might find better ways of finding common cause with them and thereby stem the tide of declining alumni support. In fact, the more ways you find to listen to your constituents and to show them that their voice is valued, that their experience matters, and that their good works in other endeavors are admired and appreciated by you, the stronger the community of purpose you will build and the more it will sustain and enhance those purposes over time. The most effective deans will be those in a constant feasibility study mode.

Campaign Planning

Chances are you will not be planning a stand-alone campaign for your school/college. If you are moving toward or are already in a campaign, it will be most likely as a part of a larger university effort or, at least, working in coordination with other institutional imperatives. In preparing for or seeking to strengthen your hand in a campaign, you don't need to worry about what portion of the campaign total you are projected to be. Internal portion allocation does not determine external market response. In other words, the deans who best attend to the principles laid out in this book, who offer the marketplace of private supporters with the clearest and most compelling conception of how private support can yield the most tangible gains in areas that are most relevant to donors' concerns will outperform expectations. Most campaigns meet their dollar goals, primarily because they are designed to avoid failure; yet, many of the categories within those campaigns will fall short. The university creates the menu of fundraising objectives, but the marketplace decides on the allocation of support. Effective deans work within the university system but expend their greatest efforts on aligning—adroitly, legitimately, and without pandering—to relevant and enabling market realities.

Campaign Management

The ubiquity and the staging of back-to-back campaigns have clouded their highest and best purpose, which is to define and rally support around unique and propitious moments. These moments happen when the assets of an institution seem perfectly poised to correspond with a major, emerging external opportunity and it is readily apparent how significant investment can be parlayed into greater institutional leadership and societal gain. Campaigns are supposed to stand in clear contrast to everyday fundraising; they are supposed to be more strategically focused to ensure that new support drives the most relevant initiatives farther down the line. They are supposed to represent a greater concentration and dedication of effort for everyone involved, most especially the senior officers of the institution. They should, like a material or political campaign, be designed and implemented to achieve concrete objectives. There should be no ambiguity about what constitutes ambiguity.

Yes, much of that is lost in the modern off-the-shelf campaign, but you can distinguish your school and your leadership in any campaign if you commandeer those larger purposes. The subtext of every successful campaign is one of institutional momentum, of a growing feeling among a larger number of internal and external constituents that the institution is picking up speed on its way to a promised land. The more assiduously you plan, the more genuinely you seek to align internal aspirations with current and emerging external realities, the more clearly you define where and how private support can make a tangible and lasting difference, and the better you communicate where and how that can increasingly happen, the more you can engineer this sense of gathering institutional momentum.

Perspective

Our philanthropic soil is rich. It has supported a number of worthy institutions and causes for hundreds of years. Each year, more and more nonprofits are created with the hope that there are still ample nutrients in it. Each year, more institutions of higher learning announce larger fundraising aspirations with the assumption that their yield will be greater. All manner of seeds seem to grow from it. All sorts of innovations seem to work on it, and many of us take credit for what it produces. Yet, we know there is a human tendency to take "natural resources" for granted, to assume that there will be more for the taking and to congratulate ourselves for getting more out of them.

We would be wise to pay attention to the early signs of erosion, particularly the number of otherwise philanthropic alumni pulling away from their alma maters, and the remarkably generous donors who wonder aloud if their accumulative giving has made a real difference. We would be wise to enrich the soil with a gratitude for its richness and with greater care for what we plant in it and hope to harvest from it. Rather than dwelling on the tactics, techniques, and, yes, gimmicks of harvesting, we would increase the chances of having abundant, upcoming harvests by cultivating enriching, sustainable conditions.

The soil will continue to produce wonders, particularly for those who continue to afford it the greatest respect.

A KEY RESOURCE

Your DO—or your president—may be interested in the book *Comprehensive Fundraising Campaigns: A Guide for Presidents and Boards*, where I outline how institutional leaders need to update their approach to running a modern comprehensive campaign.

You can order copies of that book here:

https://www.academicimpressions.com/product/comprehensive-fundraising-campaigns-guide-presidents-boards/

Appendix B: Naming Opportunities—A Word of Warning

Have you inherited a school/college without a donor's name attached to it, or are you and your faculty in one or more buildings that are similarly unadorned? Might you be thinking that those as well as many other internal spaces might constitute naming opportunities? And, further, might you be thinking that all of them give you a great philanthropic advantage? If so, hold on for a second. One of the best and most sobering exercises you engage in is to Google "naming opportunities" and observe how many of them, advertised by so many institutions of higher learning, are available. Take a random sample and see if you can find out when they were first posted. Chances are most of them were posted years ago and most of them remain "opportunities."

The wholesale offering of "naming opportunities" simply does not work. Distributing a list of buildings or programs that you are willing to name at a particular price is, quite simply, counter-philanthropic. In other words, the practice is not only inept and ineffective; it undercuts institutional dignity and, as a result, diminishes its perceived philanthropic stature. Let's consider why this is so. Throughout time, what do human societies assign the most value to? That which is most rare. The rarer the element, the commodity, the privilege, or the access to a social group, the more we prize it. I'm not arguing this is the way life should be, only the way it is. If institutions of higher learning seek to distinguish themselves through highly selective admissions, awarding precious slots to only the most accomplished and qualified students, why wouldn't they apply the same logic to their naming policies?

If a thoughtfully chosen group of donors is carefully and quietly approached, and told, quite genuinely, the institution would prefer their names on important buildings and programs because they embody the institution's highest values, a true compliment is paid in the process of soliciting gifts. And, when an institution announces and confers a donor's name on one of its structures or programs, explaining how that donor is exemplary of what the institution stands for, the institution and donor are viewed with higher esteem. Yes, most people understand that money was a part of the consideration but they also know the institution didn't just shop around the honor either.

Imagine, for instance, if you were trying to raise money for a new business school building. You could disseminate a list of naming opportunities to try to attract a set of donors who might like to see their names prominently displayed or you could ask which business leaders possess the personal and professional qualities you would most like to see manifest in your graduates. You could then approach these exemplary business leaders saying that you would like this new structure, and next phase of your business school programming, "to be built on the example of the most ethical and effective business leaders in the community, like you." You might do that by creating a "business hall of fame" in the atrium of the building with busts and personal histories of no more than five remarkable leaders (the fewer the honorees, the greater the distinction). You might also add the business school would also like to be the repository for the oral histories and professional papers of these five critical figures so that business school students of the future could continue to learn from their successes. You could approach the business leaders themselves, or the chairs of their boards, or their closest associates, or their widows and children with confidence and an easy conscience knowing you were trying to do the right thing in the right way. That's the difference between expedient, short-term fundraising and practicing true philanthropy.

But even when taking this thoughtful and genuine approach, please remember that no true philanthropist makes a considerable donation just to see his or her name on a structure or program. They want their name associated with something of lasting value. You must, therefore, make a compelling case for how the requested funds are to be used. You must make it clear that it is not just about a building itself but about the people and programs it will empower, the higher level of service it will make possible, and the enduring impact these new initiatives will have. You can't just say it; you, and the institution you represent, must be prepared and determined to live to your word.

No true philanthropist makes a considerable donation just to see his or her name on a structure or program.

No it's not about "naming opportunities," but about what your name and reputation stand for in selecting the names of those you can stand by and with over a long time.

Appendix C: Hiring the Right Development Officer

If you find yourself in search of a new DO, keep in mind several factors:

- There's a shortage of talent in the field as the size of development staffs at major institutions have grown steadily over the past three decades and the number of nonprofits have proliferated.

- Most DOs, even those with modest skills and a few years of experience, receive lots of calls from recruiters or find lots of opportunities listed in places like the *Chronicle of Higher Education* or the *Chronicle of Philanthropy*.

- The average tenure for a DO is just under two years, but conscientious practitioners are loathe to jump around because they understand the importance of sustaining prospect relations over time.

- "Success has a thousand fathers"—so for every eye-popping gift secured or highly successful campaign, there will be no shortage of gift officers claiming credit. The key is to find those who were actually instrumental in those successes. The best in the business rarely take sole credit for any gift. Instead, they will describe what they did in their time, building on the contributions of their predecessors, to help prospects find the right way and opportunity to give.

- The best gift officers did not seek to make a career in fundraising; they were attracted to causes or higher purposes early in their career, and aligned with an organization or school because they believed in the service it provided to society, so much so that they were willing to accept the responsibility for fundraising. The best way to identify and recruit the best, therefore, is by speaking to those higher purposes and how you, in your time, seek to advance them in concrete and lasting ways.

So if you want to attract the most qualified candidates, don't just put together a job description. Instead, write a case for support for your school, and describe your hopes and ambitions for advancing its mission and enhancing its impact. Don't make it look like you're looking for an employee who you can transfer all responsibility to and hold to impossibly high expectations; make it clear that you are willing to lead and accept your responsibilities, and to find someone who will work in a complementary way with you.

As you review candidates, look for the following key items on their resumes.

Career Characteristics

Long Tenures

There's a huge contradiction in the development officer who acknowledges the importance of building and sustaining relationships with prospects and donors yet jumps from place to place every couple of years. In the case of young development officers, you may see shorter tenures, which could be a sign of that person working his or her way up the career ladder. If that is the case, you should see evidence of more significant responsibility with each career move. If a DO is moving every two years or less into similar positions, it could mean he or she is simply ducking out when the bill for one's performance comes due, which should be around the two-year mark since significant gifts take, on average, twenty- one months to raise.

For more mature DOs, you should see tenures of no less than five years. However, you should also be a bit hesitant about candidates who have only worked one place and/or for their alma mater for their entire career. Yes, they may be stellar candidates who will do a fine job for you, but it is a common mistake to recruit someone from a well-developed, high-functioning advancement office in which DOs have the luxury of working with deeply grateful, continuously engaged, loyally contributing alumni of significant means, some of whom may be second generation or more, and assume that they can post similar successes at institutions that have precious few alumni who fit that bill.

Reasonable Credit Taking

If a DO, particularly in a position two or more layers removed from the vice president of advancement, takes sole credit for a string of seven-figure successes, or sole credit for single mega-gifts, your credulity should start to feel strained. Even in cases where DOs have done magnificent work, it is highly unlikely that it was a solo act (and the donor always deserves more credit than the development officer). Resumes of high achievers will speak to more specific achievements and put them in the context of what they did with what they inherited.

Succinctness

Don't expect the resume of a DO to look like the CV of a faculty member. DO resumes should be 2-3 pages in length and should succinctly describe the before and after of each position they've held. Remember, an effective DO will be able to engage prospects, particularly in the early stages of development, with succinct and compelling concepts about the cause and purpose your college/school represents. Imagine, for instance, making a call to a prospect who works on Wall Street. In such cases, the DO has no more than ten minutes to cause a frenetically busy person to want to hear more, then or later.

Cover Letter

If you want an early indication of how well prospective DOs can make a convincing case for support, see how well they do in making a case for themselves with the combination of their resume and cover letter. The resume should be a clear and impressive summary of accumulated skills and career accomplishments (not just titles, duties, and functions) while the cover letter should relate, in specific and logical ways, how those skills and accomplishments relate directly to the challenges and opportunities incumbent in the position you are offering.

Sustained, Substantive Success

Lots of development professionals can relate their success to all sorts of things, including gimmicks. You can attend fundraising conferences and hear about cleverly phased or creatively designed birthday cards to donors, or thank you videos featuring all sectors of the campus community, that were streamed to donors. You will hear about DOs who held to strict metrics of annual performance and those given the luxury of building relationships over several years. You will hear about student philanthropy events employing social media, which engendered record results in terms of dollar amounts and percentages of participation. In fact, you will hear about any number of policies, practices, and innovations, all claiming to have achieved new levels of success. And it's highly likely they did—even when a successful practice in one place seems to have contradicted with the success in another place. In a highly fertile philanthropic soil, all sorts of seeds may germinate and all sorts of crops may grow.

We shouldn't confuse cause and effect. People give because they are innately generous and they can be prompted to give in all sorts of ways. So, in reviewing resumes, look for those who have studied the agronomy of North American philanthropy (or the culture in which you live) and learned what works best across a variety of microclimates. Look for those who understand what makes people in many places want to give and who have proven that they understand. They will have proven this by the substantive achievements they've posted in different places, most especially in places that had not enjoyed such harvests before.

Ideal Human Dimensions

After you have screened the field of prospective DO candidates and prepared yourself to interview the finalists, look for the evidence of the following:

Curiosity

This quality manifests in many ways, including the intensity with which one listens, the earnestness with which one raises questions (as if it is very important for them to know the answer, that they are genuinely eager to learn, and that they are pleased, intrigued, and/or grateful for the knowledge received), the way one sits, and the body language they exhibit. The candidates that put you most at ease, that cause you to expand on topics, that make you feel respected and appreciated, and that leave you wanting to spend time with them, are the most likely to do the same for your prospects. Indeed, there is no more important skill than this. The DO candidate that does the best job of interviewing you is the one you should give the greatest consideration to.

Conviction

No DO can sustain success without believing in the cause or purpose he or she represents. In your interviews, ask your finalists why the disciplines represented by your school/college are attractive and motivating to them. Ask them how those disciplines have improved the human condition over time and how they might do so in the future. Don't hire a fundraiser who simply enjoys fundraising, because that enjoyment is not enough to sustain their efforts; there will be times when the challenges the fundraiser faces, including internal politics, will seem to outweigh the satisfaction of the work. Instead, hire a fundraiser who is motivated by mission, by making a difference where the world most needs one to be made.

Composition

Lone wolves, control freaks and those with their elbows frozen in the out position do not make the best DOs. Their successes are often short-term and come with a lot of collateral damage. Successful fundraising requires good judgment including knowing when to be present with a prospect and when to work behind the scenes, when to insist on being the primary prospect manager and when to hand that prospect off to someone else, and when to give and take credit. Those qualities are more apt to manifest in people who are personally secure.

Conscientiousness

The best DOs won't work for you alone, or your school, college or university. They will work toward an alignment of purposes between you and those that have and might support you. They know there are no such things as "gifts." Even when donors give anonymously and with restriction, their gifts come with moral obligations. Your school/college must live up to the implicit or explicit promises in your over-arching case for support and individual proposals. The living up to moral obligations renews and enriches the philanthropic soil. The best DOs don't want to mislead anyone or secure support under false or unsupportable premises. It's not because they're dreamers but because they know that principle is pragmatic. They don't want to do anything that undermines their credibility or yours or that of the institution. They know the preservation and enhancement of credibility is the compounded interest of philanthropy.

If, after interviewing your finalists, you find yourself torn between a veteran DO with several decades of experience, who falls slightly short on ideal human dimensions (curiosity, conviction, composition, and conscientiousness) and someone who lacks experience but is rich with these qualities. Or you must choose between a journeyman insider and a highly intuitive, engaging outsider, go with the raw talent. The tactics and techniques of the business can be learned quickly; the judgment to know when and how to apply them can never be taught.

And, finally, the criterion that will allow you to make the very best decision is self-knowledge. The more objective you are about what you do well and not so well, what settings you feel more and less comfortable in, and how well you listen and interact with others (and where you fall short), the more able you will be to hire your complement or close approximation thereof. The most effective fundraising deans and DOs are those that operate within the most complementary teams. **Between the two members of the team there must be a core skill set that includes:**

- Vision

- Strategic Antenna

- Courage of Conviction

- Patient Persistence

- Direction Setting

- Expectation Setting/Managing

- Subject Matter Expertise

- Listening Ability and Hearing Comprehension

- Considerateness

- Market Research Orientation

- Coalition Development

- Emotional Intelligence

- Verbal Clarity

- Written Clarity

- Task Orientation

- Time Management

- Social Ease

Since your constituents will expect that some of the skills (vision, direction setting, subject-matter expertise) must reside primarily with the dean, the DO must publicly cede those qualities to the dean.

The dean should cede to the DO those skills that constituents most expect of *that* position, most especially the setting of fundraising expectations.

IN-DEPTH TRAINING RESOURCES

Make sure to also pursue the conferences, webcasts, workshops, and articles on institutional advancement available at Academic Impressions:

https://www.academicimpressions.com

ABOUT THE AUTHOR

JAMES M. LANGLEY

Founder and President, Langley Innovations

Before forming his own comprehensive advancement consulting firm, Jim served as vice president for advancement at Georgetown University. At Georgetown, he led the institution's offices of alumni affairs, strategic communications and marketing, development, medical center development, and advancement services. During his tenure, he produced record numbers in new commitments and dollars, despite a difficult economy. He also launched a number of innovative programs, including the acclaimed Student Discovery Initiative.

Jim arrived at Georgetown after spending eight years as the vice president for advancement at the University of California, San Diego. At UCSD, he led the planning and execution of the institution's seven- year $1 billion campaign, then raised almost half the target amount in three years, despite a weak economy. Jim also previously served as vice president for external affairs at Georgia Institute of Technology, increasing annual gift income from $26 million to $76 million and more than tripling the institution's endowment to well over $500 million. Operations under his management have won awards in virtually every area of university advancement.

Made in the
USA
Columbia, SC